Technology and Human Existence:

José Ortega y Gasset's *Meditation on Technology*

by Oswald Sobrino

To Elena Sobrino, a doctoral student of technology at MIT

Contents

Preface

This book is the third in a series written by me on the philosophy of José Ortega y Gasset (1883-1955). The first book is *Freedom and Circumstance: Philosophy in Ortega y Gasset* (2011), a basic introduction to the thought of Ortega. The second book is *Philosophy in Don Quixote: Commentary on the Meditations of Ortega y Gasset* (2015), which comments on the first book published by Ortega in 1914. Both preceding books are short, inexpensive, and helpfully frame this new book; but they are not essential for the reader taking up this latest volume. All the books are available at Amazon.com (whose technology has made their publication possible).

The kernel of Ortega's philosophy that runs throughout his many books, essays, and articles is that a particular human life is something to be made and is not merely given. This insight runs throughout many other existentialist philosophers. What sets Ortega apart is a much greater clarity that avoids the obfuscating jargon and density of much continental philosophy. Ortega's philosophy is at times referred to as "vitalism" because it arises from our experience of life and always refers to the task of living. Thus, his philosophy does not need to be "made practical." It is by nature and design intrinsically practical and is marked by the clarity necessary for *praxis*.

Technology, more than ever before, flows through our daily lives and can even come to dominate it. We now carry in our palms a combination of a clock, calendar, movie theater, library, and telephone with instant and continuous access to events and people around the globe. Think of those who passed away in the nineties; they would be utterly dumbstruck at what we now take for granted. As a result of this wonder, we have less time to read entire books and spend more time cut off from social interaction and physical activity. We become more like the machines we created.

With the advent of the artificial intelligence revolution (AIR), further changes are in store that will continue to recompose the texture of daily human life. Many minds today are rightly focusing on what the AIR will mean for human existence. A prominent example comes to mind. The Massachusetts Institute of Technology (MIT) recently announced the opening of a new College of Computing "to address the global opportunities and challenges presented by the ubiquity of computing—across industries and academic disciplines—and by the rise of artificial intelligence."[1]

MIT is considered by many as one of the top global universities; one well-known college ranking organization has rated it as the number one global university for several years in a row.[2] Thus, what happens at MIT will not stay at MIT. Other global universities, in one form or another, will end up adopting and adapting what MIT pioneers in the looming AIR. The first chapter of this book takes up what kind of university the new technology is creating in 2019, since Ortega presciently took up this question in the context of 1933.

MIT's dramatic choice to recompose itself for the AIR has naturally led to great internal debate and discussion at the institute, both planned and unplanned.[3] This debate is not surprising since MIT is also home to vigorous humanities and social science programs.[4] Ortega engaged in this technology debate back in 1933. This book examines how Ortega's insights can shape today's technology debates that continue to grow and spread.

This book considers technology and human existence based on Ortega's series of lectures published as *Meditation on Technology*. I translate quotations from Ortega's book directly from the Spanish original found in the following edition: José Ortega y Gasset, *Meditación de la Técnica* (Madrid: Revista de Occidente en Alianza Editorial, 1982; originally published 1933). I cite this original Spanish edition as "MT." I am not aware of an English translation. To aid readers who wish to reference the Spanish original, my Chapters 1 through 5 comment on Ortega's Chapters 1 through 5, respectively, in MT. My Chapter 6 comments on Ortega's Chapters 6, 7,

---

[1] "FAQ on the newly established MIT Stephen A. Schwarzman College of Computing," MIT News Office, Oct. 15, 2018, available at http://news.mit.edu/2018/faq-mit-stephen-schwarzman-college-of-computing-1015 .

[2] See QS World University Rankings 2019, at https://www.topuniversities.com/university-rankings/employability-rankings/2019 .

[3] See https://shass.mit.edu/news/news-2019-ethics-computing-and-ai-perspectives-mit .

[4] In fact, Times Higher Education recently rated MIT as second in its arts and humanities ranking. See https://www.timeshighereducation.com/world-university-rankings/2019/subject-ranking/arts-and-humanities#!/page/0/length/25/sort_by/rank/sort_order/asc/cols/stats .

and 8 in MT. My Chapter 7 comments on Ortega's Chapters 9, 10, 11, and 12 in MT. The footnote citations enable readers to precisely reference MT.

"Without technology, the human being would not exist nor would ever have existed."[5] So Ortega declares in the introduction to his book *Meditation on Technology* (1933; henceforth "MT"). Ortega begins by considering the university and its relation to technology. If, to use Ortega's word, **technology is "consubstantial" with the human**, then its exclusion or depreciation within the university would be inherently obtuse and contradict the catholic (in the sense of universal) agenda of a true university.

We have come a long way from 1933. Today, the panic in certain college departments is that STEM is wiping out the arts, the humanities, and the softer social sciences. Let us return to MIT. Borrowing, as is well-known, from the European model of the polytechnic university, MIT arose to address the shift that the Boston elites sensed in the world in the mid-nineteenth century: the shift from quaint seminary-style universities for upper-class gentlemen to universities as engines of industrial and scientific research.[6] Yet, MIT, as our convenient example of technological change, is also carrying out another experiment: the interdisciplinary entanglement of the arts, humanities, and social sciences with the insights of computing, AI, and the hard sciences. Ortega would likely approve.

Yet, today, there remain large pockets of the liberal arts that exist as if technology is an alien world. Important work is indeed taking place in what is called "digital humanities" that add the power of computer searching to the humanistic exploration of the literary and historical corpus of past centuries. Yet, the attention to technology itself as an area of human inquiry is often

---

[5] José Ortega y Gasset, *Meditación de la Técnica* (Madrid: Revista de Occidente en Alianza Editorial, 1982; originally published 1933). All translations from the original Spanish are mine. I translate the generic "*hombre*" ("man") as human or human being. As noted in my preface, "MT" stands for this particular edition of *Meditación de la Técnica* (*Meditation on Technology*).

[6] See Letter from William Barton Rogers (MIT founder) to His Brother Henry, March 13, 1846, at https://libraries.mit.edu/archives/timeline/letter1846.html ; A.J. Angulo, *William Barton Rogers and the Idea of MIT* (Baltimore: The Johns Hopkins University Press, 2009), p. 88; Elizabeth Andrews, Nora Murphy, and Tom Rosko, "William Barton Rogers: MIT's Visionary Founder," at https://libraries.mit.edu/archives/exhibits/wbr-visionary/index.html .

relegated to specialized fields such as STS (Science and Technology in Society). This continuing lack of a broader humanities focus on technology makes Ortega's lament still relevant.

Yet, the problem runs in both directions. Ortega criticizes both economists who ignore the impact of technology and the social questions it raises and engineers who do likewise.[7] Anticipating C.P. Snow's famous 1959 lecture[8] on the split between the humanities and the sciences, Ortega laments:

> In sum, the radical separation of the university and engineering is one of the greatest calamities fostering the incredible inertia that modern humans display in response to great, present-day tragedies. This separation is fatal, for different but complementary reasons, for the university and for engineering.[9]

Interestingly, Ortega presents the modern university's relation to technology as worse than that of the medieval university because so much of our much more extensive modern technology is so distant from everyday human familiarity. Ortega notes how the medieval person, for example, observed daily the obvious workings of agricultural instruments and the care of livestock while modern persons "[rarely] see [their] corresponding technologies in action because, for the most part, they are invisible, that is, their observable appearance does not uncover their reality and make them intelligible."[10]

This invisibility of modern technology itself creates "a new and gigantic problem."[11] MIT and those universities which will follow its anticipated path-breaking approach will actively engage their humanists, artists, and social scientists in facing, for example, the AI revolution precisely to uncover and make visible the potential social complications and consequences of

---

[7] MT, 15. All cited numbers refer to pages.
[8] C.P. Snow, *The Two Cultures* (Cambridge, UK: Cambridge University Press, 2012; reissued by Canto Classics).
[9] MT, 15.
[10] MT, 16.
[11] MT, 17.

frighteningly and impressively powerful technologies. **Ortega's insight gives us a way to name the necessary task of universities:** *to make visible what is already underway.* The anthropologist, sociologist, and economist can make visible the effects of new technologies on social class, on economic opportunity, and on environmental health. Literary, philosophical, and theological scholars can make visible the psychological and ethical deformations that should be avoided and those new ethical advances that can be embraced. The work of such humanistic scholars will be wasted if the inventors, the engineers, the technologists, and the "hard" scientists do not participate directly in making technology visible. In other words, our traditional view of discrete, "siloed" academic research is now more irrelevant than ever. The complication and power of new technologies have torn down the silos.

As usual, there is a political dimension to such a massive undertaking of making things visible. Political scientists, lawyers, and public officials must make the role of government and of large corporations visible so that the development and implementation of new technologies can be transparent to democratic control. The tragedy of Facebook, for example, lies in the combination of tremendous control over the daily lives of millions hidden in the entrails of a private corporation. The constant exposure of Facebook's misuse of its technological power highlights how primitively invisible the operation of an inherently social technology can be in the current corporate model. Corporate and accounting scholars in law and business must develop ways to increasingly "socialize" the private corporation that wields such vast social power. In addition, the role of Russia in the 2016 U.S. election was a surprise for many and thus another example of the power of invisible technology that also requires the focus of national security experts.

As you can see from this inventory of university scholars whose work is needed to make technology's role visible, the entire university is implicated. Even in my own field of Greco-Roman Classical Studies, there is work to do. A pivotal example is the topic of slavery. The ancient world accepted with little controversy the idea of natural slavery, as championed by the great polymath and scientist Aristotle. To what extent, are modern technologies of surveillance, advertising, and control creating a new, modern slavery taken for granted because of its invisibility? It is arguable that those controlled and deceived by modern technology are being transformed into the "slaves by

6

nature" that Aristotle described and accepted as normal. Even the Hellenist and Latinist can contribute to our understanding of how modern subservience to technology shares many traits with ancient slavery by creating and resting upon an easily manipulated population. The challenge is, to quote Ortega, "the updating of our tools and institutions."[12] It is time, as they say, to think big.

Ortega encourages optimism in this quest. The historian can remind us of the past's experience with different forms of social organizations and how they have been replaced with improved forms since, according to Ortega, "human history, examined closely in its innermost dimension, is a series of linked experiences, a dialectic of experiences."[13] This hope for the future can begin "with what is closest to us—the university. Let us attempt a new university. Exploring here, exploring there, let us try to discover more effective modes of higher education."[14]

---

[12] MT, 17.
[13] MT, 18.
[14] MT, 19.

Chapter 1: Human Needs and Necessities

Ortega proceeds by talking about human needs or necessities. His characteristic method is to assume nothing and so begins by defining basic survival needs such as the need for warmth, shelter, and food in the first chapter of MT. His first conclusion is that these needs arise from the necessity to live (*vivir*).[15] He also defines nature, the supplier of our needs, as nothing more than "what surrounds the human being, circumstance."[16] The focus on living and on circumstance reflects the two fundamental pillars of Orteguian thought, as we shall see as we progress in examining his comments on technology.

He also proceeds by contrasting the human being's relation with nature to that of the animal. Ortega suggests that, subjectively, the animal does not have "necessities," as experienced by the human being. The animal lives to feed or warm himself—that is his life. It is not a "necessity" in the human sense of something imposed as unavoidable, as a burden, which must be discharged so that the human being can survive and then proceed to pursue *other ends* that are closer to his heart.[17] Here lies the reason why Ortega views technology as consubstantial for being human: the human does not, as we colloquially say, "roll over and die" when food or warmth is lacking.[18] The human being, faced with the same obstacles as the animal to food or warmth, "engages in a new kind of doing that consists in producing what was not previously present in nature."[19] Even more radically different from the animal, the human being is also "capable of temporarily distancing himself

---

[15] MT, 24.

[16] MT, 25.

[17] MT, 26-27.

[18] MT, 25.

[19] MT, 25. I do not share Ortega's implied tendency to view the non-human animal as lacking technology. In my view, the beaver, for example, clearly uses technology (building a convenient lodge, building a dam) to secure his need for shelter and food (see Alina Bradford, "Facts About Beavers," Oct. 13, 2015, https://www.livescience.com/52460-beavers.html). The distinction between the animal's technology and that of the human seems more a matter of degree than of the presence *vel non* (or not) of technology itself. This continuity in technology between the human animal and the non-human animal is consistent with Ortega's view of the human as part of nature or circumstance.

from his urgent survival needs . . . in order to be free to pursue other activities that in themselves do not seek to satisfy these necessities."[20]

From these considerations, Ortega begins to sketch the core of his philosophical perspective:

> The animal cannot withdraw from his repertoire of animal acts, from nature, because the animal is nature and would have no place to go if he distanced himself from nature. But the human being, as just seen, is not his circumstance, but is only immersed in his circumstance and can on some occasions exit his circumstance, withdraw into himself, enter into himself (*"ensimismarse"*) and, alone, devote himself to things that do not directly or immediately address the imperatives and necessities of his circumstance."[21]

The result is that the human can then "build a fire, build a house, cultivate fields, and invent a car."[22] In this way, technology arises. Ortega defines technology as "the reformation that the human being imposes on nature to satisfy his necessities," which in effect creates a new nature (*"sobrenaturaleza"*).[23] The human being "imposes . . . a change upon nature" in order to render necessities null and void because their satisfaction is no longer problematic."[24] Ortega emphasizes that technology is not the mere satisfaction of necessities but the imposition of change upon nature in order to annul the burden of unmet necessities.[25]

---

[20] MT, 26.
[21] MT, 27.
[22] MT, 27.
[23] MT, 28.
[24] MT, 28.
[25] MT, 28.

Chapter 2: Human Well-Being

Although I disagree with Ortega's view of the animal as completely alien to technology,[26] I fully agree with Ortega's definition of technology itself: "Technology is the contrary of the agent adapting to its environment, instead technology is the adaptation of the environment to the agent."[27] What is especially noteworthy thus far in Ortega's discussion is his view of technology as integral to human nature: "A human being without technology, that is, one without a response to his environment, is not a human being."[28] Here again we see that in Ortega's creed the human being is consubstantial with technology as he defines it.

Yet, Ortega takes a surprising turn, surprising to those of us who view technology as eminently practical and utilitarian. Ortega proposes that technology, from its primitive beginnings, does not merely seek to satisfy needs necessary for survival but also seeks to satisfy forms of pleasure. He gives the examples of music and of substances specifically used to attain a state of psychological well-being and exaltation (*"embriaguez"*).[29] He notes the possibility that the bow was first a musical instrument before becoming a weapon for hunting and warfare.[30] He makes these points to refine our definition of a necessity for human beings, a definition that he considers crucial for usefully thinking about technology:

> These considerations [just noted above] reveal that the primitive human being did not view certain states of pleasure any less necessary than obtaining the minimum necessary to avoid death; as a result, from the beginning, the concept of

---

[26] See my comments in note 19 above.
[27] MT, 31.
[28] MT, 32.
[29] MT, 32.
[30] See MT, 32-33.

"human necessity" has equally included the objectively necessary as well as the superfluous.[31]

As a result, Ortega proposes human well-being as "the fundamental necessity for the human being."[32] This twist on necessity changes much of our assumed perspective on human needs and technology. The art department of a university can use this view to justify its role in the eyes of unsympathetic administrators. They can point, for example, to the cave paintings of Altamira, in Ortega's own beloved Iberian Peninsula, to argue that if art was necessary for the primitive hunter who expended his comparatively meager resources for producing art then, *a fortiori*, a modern, wealthy society cannot ignore the arts in its universities. That is an important reason why a university such as MIT that is the embodiment of technology can very justifiably and logically boast of its commitment to the arts.[33]

At this point, we should linger on the admittedly paradoxical nature, as Ortega himself points out, of what has just been asserted. Ortega states this paradox in a challenging way: "[F]or the human being, the objectively superfluous is the only thing necessary. . . . And this is essential for understanding technology. Technology is the production of the superfluous: both today and in the paleolithic era."[34] Nevertheless, Ortega insists again on the great difference between the animal and the human: the animal is merely looking for survival and not for well-being, while for the human being "technology and well-being are, in the end, synonymous."[35] Again, I find the Orteguian insistence on the gap between animal and human overdone: even the humble beaver seeks well-being by including a convenient, underwater entrance to his lodge![36] My guess is that Ortega is seeking to affirm how essential technology is to human identity by emphasizing the contrast with other animals. Yet, the identity of the human being as also an animal and as part of the animal kingdom can be used to bolster the argument for the

---

[31] MT, 33.
[32] MT, 33.
[33] See https://arts.mit.edu/cast/ .
[34] MT, 34-35.
[35] MT, 35.
[36] See the link cited in note 19 above.

essential role of technology in being human: if other animals also enjoy technology for their own survival and well-being, how much more does this further anchor technology as essential in the makeup of that other, higher functioning animal: the human.

Returning to the definition of technology, we see that Ortega adds this corollary to his view of technology as based on human well-being: since human definitions of well-being are variable and subjective, technology itself will be characterized by the same variability and malleability—"a protean reality, in constant mutation."[37] This constant mutation is beyond dispute.

Ortega also infers that this variability in what is desired as well-being produces in history the reality of abandoned and lost technologies and the reality that some inventors and inventions have been feared and that some inventors have even been persecuted.[38] Certainly, even the physicists involved in the birth of nuclear weapons came to harbor great fear about them. Moreover, many have wished for a long time for the complete abandonment of such weapons, however unlikely the prospect after their diffusion throughout the world. Clearly, today many also fear the AI revolution as dehumanizing, destabilizing, and dangerous.

---

[37] MT, 36.
[38] MT, 37.

Ch. 3: Existing as Human

Ortega entitles his third chapter with the declaration that "The Effort to Save Labor is Technology." He also begins this third chapter with a digression which is of vital importance today, as in 1933: the fragility and mutability of technology. Ortega warns that it takes only a change in the idea of human well-being ("*bienestar*") for the traditional technology to "collapse and take other paths."[39] An even eerier warning follows, especially eerie in the Europe of 1933 with the rise of Hitler:

> Progressivism [read: the Enlightenment] in assuming that it had arrived at a historical level from which there would be no substantial regression and which would mechanically advance without end, weakened the underpinnings of human caution and has permitted the eruption of a new barbarism in the world.[40]

Let's not mince words: many sense that the same eruption of barbarism is happening through right-wing, populist movements in both the United States and in Europe. Ortega would not be surprised at all. To see a president of the United States winking at pro-Nazi demonstrators and laughing at the suggestion that illegal immigrants should be shot is something that many of us never expected to witness after the Civil Rights Movement and the court rulings and congressional legislation that codified the gains of that movement. Ortega warned then and warns now that barbarism is easily restored. Even those of us who temperamentally prefer to avoid overreacting to events and trends cannot ignore or downplay what is happening.

In terms of technology, we can say that, parallel to such political trends, the established use of technology to advance human well-being can be twisted to advance a form of human well-being defined by racism and xenophobia through totalitarian surveillance, control, and brainwashing. Technology can easily become a force for evil and cease to be the great liberator of humanity.

---

[39] MT, 40.
[40] MT, 40.

All such fears are consistent with Ortega's main point about the character of technology as a historical phenomenon: **"[T]echnology varies to the highest degree and is supremely unstable, depending on the idea of well-being that humans embrace on any particular occasion."**[41]

Ortega then summarily restates his view of technology as the activity 1.) that assures the "satisfaction" of basic needs; 2.) that achieves that goal "with minimum effort" on the part of human beings; and 3.) that creates "completely new possibilities" in the human environment.[42] Ortega focuses on the first two parts of his definition of technological activity, the parts that are concerned with the labor-saving aspect of technology.

Ortega in 1933 foresees the central problem of what humans will do with the newly available time made available by technology: "if with technology humans are freed from the tasks imposed by nature, what will humans then do, what tasks will occupy their lives?"[43] It is now a commonplace observation in the 21st century that advanced technological societies need to consider instituting a universal basic income to take care of the economic needs of citizens whose labor is no longer needed, whose labor has made been redundant by technology.

Ortega asserts that this human freedom from the pressing work of survival in nature is what distinguishes humans from the other animals who remain trapped in the survival mode.[44] In this vacuum created by time saved from tasks required for survival, humans "dedicate themselves to a series of non-biological tasks . . . that they themselves invent . . . . And *that* invented life, invented as one creates a novel or a play, is what humans call human life and well-being."[45] At this point, Ortega repeats the statement that is a hallmark of the existentialist philosopher: life is not given to humans as it is to a rock or to an animal—instead humans invent their lives and become "novelists of themselves" and use technology for that end.[46]

---

[41] MT, 41.
[42] MT, 42.
[43] MT, 42-43.
[44] MT, 43.
[45] MT, 43-44 (emphasis added).
[46] MT, 44.

What is of special interest to us today is that Ortega (and we also) cannot analyze technology without philosophizing about what it means to be human. Thinking about technology is impossible without a philosophical anthropology. This result is consistent with the Orteguian view previously presented: technology is "consubstantial" with our humanity and not an extracurricular activity.

Ch. 4: Programming Human Life

The title of this chapter does not refer to a mad scientist programming a modern Frankenstein. Rather, according to Ortega, "programming" human life is what humans have always done from the beginning of time. First, Ortega sets the stage with what he calls "the most radical phenomenon of all . . . that our existing consists in being surrounded as much by things favorable to us as by difficulties."[47] He affirms that this "intricate network" of the favorable and the difficult "gives to the reality we call human life its special ontological character."[48]

Again, we see the contrast between human living and the proverbial rock in a passage that captures the heart of Ortega's view of human life, a life which has technology as one of its intrinsic constituents:

> Note well: existence is given ready-made to the rock without the rock struggling to be what it is: a rock in the landscape. But for the human being existing is to incessantly struggle with the difficulties of his environment; therefore, it is a matter of constructing, in each instance, for himself ("*hacerse*") his own existence. Let us say then that for the human being the abstract possibility of existing is what is given, but not the reality of existing. The human being must capture that reality of existing, minute by minute: **the human being must earn his life ("*ganarse la vida*") not only economically but also metaphysically.**[49]

The phrase in bold print is a suitable summary of Ortega's philosophy. The usually cited summary of his philosophy is the phrase he penned in his first published work from 1914: "I am I and my circumstance; and if I do not

---

[47] MT, 45.
[48] MT, 46-47.
[49] MT, 46-47 (emphasis added).

save it, I cannot save myself."[50] If my circumstance is part of my "I," then it is clear that my life intrinsically involves actively relating to and colliding with my circumstance to "earn" my life.

In another telling metaphor about being human, Ortega calls the human being "a type of ontological centaur."[51] He explains that the human being is in part "natural" ("immersed . . . in nature") and "extranatural" ("transcends nature").[52] That natural part "realizes itself," while the extranatural part "consists in a life project."[53] It is this life project that we call our "authentic being"—"the intense desire (*afán*) to realize a specific project or program of existence."[54]

In this way, Ortega's philosophical anthropology parallels how we speak of software and the computer: we program a computer and thereby grant it an identity, a use, a function. The programming is the "life," so to speak, of the hardware. Likewise, our human life is that program or project that I intensely desire and pursue. Interestingly, the computer hardware derives its "life" or program from a human program invented by a human being. That is why we refer to *artificial* intelligence as opposed to human intelligence: we make the machine intelligent by sharing our intelligence. In this way, all artificial intelligence is at root the human intelligence from which it derives.

The computer program, like the rock, remains, in Ortega's terminology, a "thing" whose "being is already given and attained," even if it can learn new things.[55] In contrast, the human being is not a thing but rather "the pretension [the project] of being this or that."[56] Ortega summarizes his view of human life: "I am not a thing, but rather a drama, a struggle to be what I must be."[57] If the human is a project, then "nature" or "world" or "circumstance" is a

---

50   José Ortega y Gasset, *Meditaciones del Quijote*, Biblioteca de Cultura Básica, Ediciones de la Universidad de Puerto Rico (Madrid: Revista de Occidente, 1957), 43-44 (in Ortega's introduction).
51   MT, 47.
52   MT, 47.
53   MT, 47-48.
54   MT, 48.
55   MT, 49.
56   MT, 49.
57   MT, 49.

collection of things favoring or making difficult our life project.[58] As our life projects vary, so the nature/world/circumstance that we face itself varies with different aspects favoring or making difficult different types of life projects.[59]

Ortega shows that discussing technology presupposes that we have discussed being human. There can be no philosophy of technology without a philosophy of the human being. To plan the role of technology and to discern what to change or limit in technology requires a philosophical anthropology. Ironically, on the frontier of science, we are thrown back to the ancient art of philosophizing, which even some professional, academic philosophers have abandoned.

---

[58] MT, 49.
[59] MT, 50.

In an atypical use of metaphor, Ortega again emphasizes his central point:

> The human being, whether he desires it or not, must create himself ("*hacerse a si mismo*"), auto-produce himself ("*autofabricarse*") . . . . This [expression] highlights that the human being, at the root of his essence, finds himself, above all, in the predicament of a practitioner of technology. For the human, to live is, always and above all, to bring about the existence of what does not yet exist; namely, to bring himself into existence by using what already exists; in sum, the human being *is* production [original emphasis].[60]

For too long, there has been an assumed tension, even contradiction, between what is quintessentially human as celebrated in the humanities and what technology is. Ortega is reorienting this prejudice. It is a Copernican Revolution in the relation of the human to the technical: no longer is technology a helpful, but alien (and maybe dangerous) satellite orbiting the distinctively human. Technology is now intrinsic to human existing, and human existing is intrinsic to technology.[61] To save both the human and the technological requires the collapse of the traditional, assumed dualism.

Yet, the pre-technological retains priority: "technology is not strictly speaking first."[62] Ortega further develops this assertion: "It [technology] . . . executes the mission of life. . . . But it does not define the program . . . . The program of life is pre-technological."[63] In noting that technological invention serves to meet the needs of the human being, Ortega returns to his view of human needs which themselves "are also an invention; they [human needs] are what the human being seeks to be in each epoch, nation, or person,

---

[60] MT, 52.
[61] See MT, 52-53.
[62] MT, 54.
[63] MT, 54.

namely, a prior pre-technological invention, the greatest invention, which is **the original desire**."[64]

Let us focus on the phrase "original desire." How far can artificial intelligence go in simulating, much less duplicating, that original human desire? This original human desire is the choice and commitment to an imagined future life project that emerges from past experiences, dreams, emotions, and even rebelliousness seeking to change one's circumstance. Could a machine ever create that original human desire that brings what is authentically *res nova*, what is really new, into being?[65]

Nevertheless, Ortega also points to the improbability of authentic desire in the human being (as opposed to inauthentic desire merely imitating what the anonymous "they" impose[66]). This crisis of human desire arises because of "the lack of imagination to invent the argument of one's own life."[67] Hence, the humanities as the incubators of authentic human desires (but as reinvigorated incubators and not as stale traditionalism) are as important as ever for triggering technological development that brings about well-being (*bienestar*) and happiness (*felicidad*) for the human being.[68]

---

[64] MT, 54 (emphasis added).

[65] See MT, 55.

[66] See MT, 54-55, where Ortega mocks the *nouveau riche* who simply uses his money to buy what others socially approve.

[67] MT, 56.

[68] See MT, 56.

Ch. 6: The Variety of Human Creativity

In Chapter 6, Ortega digresses to illustrate how different human projects engender different technologies. He begins with a description of the Buddhist holy man who seeks to retreat inward from the activities and consumption of the external world. This life project therefore does not engender technologies focused on rapid travel, rapid communication, or vast, well-stocked grocery stores. In contrast, the typical modern bourgeois and worker enthusiastically seek all these things. Yet, Ortega points out that the Buddhist holy man does indeed create his own type of technology: the technology dedicated to focus, concentration, and prayer—very different technology from the usual, but still technology.[69]

Ortega also offers another Buddhist example, an example of how technology originally intended for one purpose can end up fulfilling other significant purposes. Ortega considers the spread of Buddhism in the inhospitable climate and terrain of Tibet. The meditative life of Buddhism required monasteries, permanent buildings, that the nomadic Tibetans did not use. The religious project of Buddhism led to a major transformation of the Tibetan landscape through the technology of permanent construction. Moreover, Ortega attributes to this originally religious project the ultimate rise of a Tibetan state.[70] I do not seek to verify the historicity of Ortega's Tibetan example, but simply to relate its major point: once technology imposes change on the world, there are likely to be originally unintended consequences.[71] In much the same way, European monasteries ended up preserving the ancient pagan literary culture of Rome in buildings erected, ironically, to worship the Jewish prophet executed by pagan Rome.

In contrast to the Buddhist holy man, Ortega proposes the type of the "gentleman," not as a British aristocrat but as the man of business, commerce, and the professions—the active man, including the worker, immersed in the

---

[69] MT, 58-59 (Ch. 6).

[70] MT, 60 (Ch. 6).

[71] Tibetan monasteries are still viewed as centers of Tibetan national identity as Ortega's example implies. See the summary of an April 2016 report on Tibetan monasteries at https://freetibet.org/tibets-monasteries .

affairs of the world.[72] For English-speaking ears, his use of "gentleman" sounds esoteric and peculiar. For most of us, the English gentleman is the aristocrat or one belonging to the upper class and does not include the shopkeeper or the factory worker. For this reason, I will substitute "middle class" or "bourgeois" to better capture Ortega's peculiar use of "gentleman." At least for most Americans, "middle class" can include anyone from the physician to the factory worker within a broad range of disposable income that is well above the poverty level.

Ortega's digression on the so-called "gentleman" type is a bit puzzling. But let us look more closely. In his Chapter 7, Ortega wonders if the "gentleman" type still exists in the England of the nineteen thirties, the England of the Great Depression.[73] Ortega then raises the Spanish version of the gentleman: the *hidalgo*, the Spanish nobleman who lives in poverty but somehow manages to preserve his dignity. What can we make of all of this?

Ortega's talk of gentlemen and *hidalgos* indeed sounds odd to us (as if a strange refrain from an extremely distant past). Yet, the topic does raise an important contemporary issue: how do we preserve human dignity when technology may take away the productive employment of many, whether white-collar or blue-collar? The dignified but impoverished Spanish *hidalgo* can remind us that we face choices as a society about a minimum basic income to preserve the dignity of individuals no longer needed to do mundane office work or stand in the assembly-line—or even no longer needed for basic medical, legal, or teaching tasks.

In Chapter 8 of MT, Ortega raises two very interesting points. The first concerns the fact that intelligence alone does not explain technology. Ortega points to animals as intelligent and with "the capacity . . . to produce basic instruments."[74] Yet, according to Ortega, the animal cannot produce technology because of a defective "memory, namely, the inability to preserve what recently occurred and, consequently, the meager material that is offered to its intelligence for creative combination."[75] Ortega bases his thesis of

---

[72] MT, 61-62 (the discussion of the gentleman begins in these pages in Ortega's Chapter 6 and continues into Chapter 7).
[73] MT, 65-66 (Ch. 7).
[74] MT, 69 (Ch. 8).
[75] MT, 70 (Ch. 8).

defective animal memory on chimpanzee research current in his era. However, a much more recent study (Inoue & Matsuzawa 2007)[76] concluded "that young chimpanzees have an extraordinary working memory capability for numerical recollection — better even than that of human adults tested in the same apparatus following the same procedure."

Given the diversity of the animal kingdom and the changing nature of research, we should be wary of Ortega's reference to the chimpanzee research of his time as representative of all animals. Yet, Ortega's central point can survive even if we are cautious.

Putting aside the comparisons to animals, Ortega's central point is that mere instrument-making and even mere intelligence in general are not indications of being able to create technology:

> It [intelligence] does not know on its own what, among the infinite things that can be "invented," ought to be preferred and so loses itself in its infinite possibilities. Only in a being in whom intelligence serves imagination—a non-technological imagination creating life projects—can technological capacity exist.[77]

A second interesting point in Ortega's Chapter 8 is the need to consider the historical stages of technology so we can understand the qualitatively different role of technology in the modern world compared to its role in the pre-historic and proto-historic world and its role in the West's classical and medieval worlds.[78] This second point leads us to the next and last chapter of this book.

---

[76] "Working memory of numerals in chimpanzees":
https://www.sciencedirect.com/science/article/pii/S096098220702088X .
[77] MT, 70 (Ch. 8).
[78] MT, 71 (Ch. 8).

Ch. 7: Three Stages of Technology

In considering the stages of technology, Ortega makes two points. First, that "everything that I have been saying in this course [of lectures] seeks to correct the typical error that fixates on this or that invention as what is significant in technology."[79] Instead Ortega asserts that the vital or life project preceding and triggering the technology is what is significant. That human context is what makes a particular technology significant. Second, Ortega points to the well-known example of how the Chinese invented gunpowder and printing well before Europeans, and yet these inventions sunk into oblivion until revived by Europeans much later within a very different socio-cultural context.[80] This second point emphasizes how technologies can become invisible or even disappear altogether.[81]

In the end, Ortega settles on this principle to determine the stages of technology: demarcate the three stages of technology according to the distinctive idea that human beings have of technology in general and of their relationship to it. Ortega's use of this subjective, social dimension in the history of technology anticipates to some degree the type of analysis of scientific history made famous by Thomas Kuhn in 1962.[82]

Ortega proposes three stages of technology:

1. Fortuitous technology;

2. Artisan technology;

3. Modern technology.[83]

---

[79] MT, 73 (Ch. 9). Henceforth, I designate the original Ortega chapter in MT corresponding to the page citation.

[80] MT, 74 (Ch. 9).

[81] MT, 73 (Ch. 9).

[82] Kuhn, *The Structure of Scientific Revolutions* (Chicago: University of Chicago Press, 1962). Interestingly, Kuhn's last university post was at MIT (1979-1991).

[83] MT, 74-75 (Ch. 9). The label used here for the third stage fully emerges in Ch. 12 of MT.

1. Fortuitous Technology

The stage of fortuitous technology is the stage in which the primitive[84] human being lacks conscious awareness of the general concept of technology as the "capacity, in principle, for unlimited change and progress."[85] In this stage, the human being views technology, such as the ability to ignite fire, as an undifferentiated part "of his repertoire of natural acts," such as "walking, swimming, hitting, etc."[86] In this sense, Ortega views the primitive human as "almost wholly pure animal."[87] This comment interestingly qualifies the impression previously given by Ortega that the non-human animal as such lacks technology. In his comment about the primitive human being, Ortega now depicts a continuity between non-human animals and primitive human beings engaging in technology. This continuity seems more defensible than a sharp division between animals allegedly without any technology versus humans with technology.[88]

What is the fortuitous dimension of this primitive technology? Ortega gives an example:

> The primitive human is not aware that he is able to invent, and because he lacks this awareness, his process of inventing is not an antecedent and deliberate search for solutions. As suggested earlier, it is more a matter of the solution finding him . . . . For example, rubbing, as a diversion or accidentally, two sticks produces fire. As a result, the primitive human

---

[84] I use the term "primitive" because Ortega uses it to refer to the earliest human beings. My use does not pejoratively and hubristically imply that the earliest human beings are, *ipso facto*, morally, spiritually, or socially inferior to us. For Ortega, this first stage corresponds to humans of the "pre-historic and proto-historic" eras, plus human tribes still at this technological stage in the modern era (MT, 75, Ch. 9). I refuse to use Ortega's dated and demeaning reference to "the current savage" (MT, 75, Ch. 9).

[85] MT, 75 (Ch. 9).

[86] MT, 75 (Ch. 9).

[87] MT, 75 (Ch. 9).

[88] See my comments at footnote 19 above concerning the discussion at MT, 25.

suddenly sees a new nexus between objects . . . . This new power, the sticks that ignite fire, gains . . . a magical aura.[89]

The key point at the stage of primitive technology is that the human being is not conscious of himself as *"homo faber,"* the human being as artisan or inventor.[90]

2. Artisan Technology

At this second stage, there is "enormous growth of technological work."[91] Nevertheless, the understanding of this technological reality is limited to the idea of the artisan who has the ability to accomplish certain tasks, whether as "a shoemaker, blacksmith, builder, leather worker, etc."[92] Ortega elaborates that the human being "still is not aware of technology as such, but is already aware that there are technicians, individuals who possess a special repertoire of activities which are nothing more than the general and natural activities of every person."[93]

Interestingly, Ortega anticipates the *stable phase* of scientific paradigms in Kuhn:

> The artisan lacks awareness of invention. The artisan must undergo a long apprenticeship . . . to learn already elaborated technologies that come from an impenetrable tradition. The artisan is inspired by the goal of incorporating himself into the tradition as such: the artisan is turned toward the past and is not open to possible innovations. Yet there are ... modifications, improvements that are not viewed as

---

[89] MT 76 (Ch. 9).

[90] MT 77 (Ch. 9).

[91] MT, 80 (Ch. 10). In European chronology, this stage corresponds to the era of Greco-Roman civilization and the Middle Ages (MT, 79, Ch. 10).

[92] MT, 80 (Ch. 10).

[93] MT, 80 (Ch. 10).

26

substantive innovations but rather as variations of style according to skill.[94]

Ortega insightfully shares another reason why the artisan stage lacks a mature conception of technology as a capacity separate from the skills of the artisan:

> Invention to this point has produced only instruments, not machines. This distinction is crucial. The first machine as such, and along with it an anticipation of the third stage, is Roberts' loom in 1825. It is the first machine because it is the first instrument that is self-acting and on its own produces the object . . . . In the world of the artisan, the utensil or instrument acts only as a supplement to the human being . . . . [who] remains the principal actor. On the other hand, in the machine . . . it is the human being who merely helps and supplements the machine.[95]

The rise of machines is what eventually triggers human awareness *in the third stage* "that technology is an activity apart from the natural human being" that, in contrast to the limitations of human activity, is, because of machinery, "in principle, unlimited."[96]

In the second stage of artisan technology, the lack of distinction in the person of the artisan between "the technician" who initiates a plan or scheme for the work at hand and "the worker" implementing these plans hides something else that will also eventually become apparent in the third stage of technology.[97] In the third stage of modern technology, the separation between the technician as planner and the worker as operator will become evident.[98]

---

[94] MT, 81 (Ch. 10).
[95] MT, 81-82 (Ch. 10).
[96] MT, 82 (Ch. 10).
[97] MT, 82 (Ch. 10).
[98] MT, 82, (Ch. 10).

3. Modern Technology

This modern conception of technology is the idea "that technology is not this or that particular, and as such fixed, technology, but is precisely the source of human activities that are, in principle, unlimited."[99]

This "new awareness of technology" puts humans beings in an entirely new situation: rather than living with the constant awareness of human limitations, now the human being can sincerely assume that no imagined achievement is necessarily unattainable or impossible.[100] Ortega gives, as an example about fifty-six years before the actual event, a potential moon landing as something that humans in 1933—with a modern appreciation of technology as unlimited—could no longer exclude.[101]

(Ortega notes in passing that this new era of unlimited technical achievement also creates a very human problem: if I can attempt anything, I must still choose something in particular to attempt; otherwise, my life becomes a vacuum.[102])

In contrast to the artisan stage, the third stage of modern technology then has these hallmarks:

1. As a result of the tremendous growth of technology, "the human being [now] cannot live without technology."[103] As confirmation of this observation, Ortega points to the enormous growth of population in Europe in the 19th and 20th centuries that was made possible by technology.[104] The issue of global warming now puts at risk this population growth and, at the same time, presents an unprecedented challenge to technology.

2. The previously noted appearance of the machine gives rise to the "factory . . . [as] an independent artifact helped on occasion by a few human

---

[99] MT, 83 (Ch. 10).
[100] MT, 83 (Ch. 10).
[101] MT, 83 (Ch. 10).
[102] MT, 83-84 (Ch. 10).
[103] MT, 85 (Ch. 11).
[104] MT, 85 (Ch. 11).

beings with a very modest role."[105] Again, the Ortega of 1933 is prescient, well before the robot revolution on the assembly line.

3. As previously noted, the third stage makes evident the separation between the roles of the technician and of the worker, roles previously combined in the single person of the artisan. Now, the role of the technician, that is, the engineer, who plans and designs technology is isolated from the role of running the machinery.[106] The technician (defined in this context as the creator of technology) is the person dedicated to the task of inventing who now consciously participates in technology as a way of life no longer hidden from view, as it was hidden for the primitive human among his natural activities or hidden for the artisan within his guild tradition.[107]

Yet, Ortega goes further in his thinking about modern technology. He seeks to isolate the methodological difference between the artisan stage of technology and the modern stage of technology. He focuses on what he calls "technicism" as "the intellectual method operating in the creation of technology."[108]

To set the stage for explaining this difference in method or "technicism," he first describes the intellectual method of the artisan, taking as an example the Egyptian architect seeking to lift huge stones in the construction of a pyramid.[109] For the Egyptian architect or technician, the search is for "means . . . [aimed] at a total, undivided, brute result." [110] Ortega describes the "technicism" or intellectual method involved: "The undifferentiated unity of the result [the goal of lifting the heavy stones to construct the pyramid] sparks the search for means that are likewise undifferentiated."[111] As a result, "the

---

[105] MT, 87 (Ch. 11).
[106] See MT, 87 (Ch. 11).
[107] See MT, 87 (Ch. 11).
[108] MT, 88 (Ch. 11).
[109] MT, 88 (Ch. 11).
[110] MT, 88 (Ch. 11).
[111] MT, 89 (Ch. 11).

means for accomplishing the result are very similar to the result."[112] The Egyptians used earth piled up "in the shape of a pyramid" as a ramp for dragging the stones to the top of the pyramid under construction.[113] Ortega views this intellectual method of using similar things for similar results as a form of the same trial and error used in the primitive stage of technology.[114]

What then is the new intellectual method of the modern stage of technology? Ortega points to 16th century Europe and specifically to Galileo (1564-1642).[115] The new method or "technicism" is **analysis**: "That is, it [the new technicism] deconstructs the total result sought . . . into the partial results from which the total result arises. In other words, [it deconstructs the total result sought] into its 'causes' or ingredients."[116] Ortega points, as an example, to Galileo's deconstruction of physical movement into its component movements.[117]

Compare this method as described by Ortega to the work of Marvin Minsky, a pioneer of AI, in his book *The Society of Mind*:

> This book tries to explain how minds work. How can intelligence emerge from nonintelligence? To answer that, we'll show that you can build a mind from many little parts, each mindless by itself. I'll call "Society of Mind" this scheme in which each mind is made of many smaller processes. These we'll call agents. **Each mental agent by itself can only do some simple thing that needs no mind or thought at all. Yet when we join these agents in societies--in certain very special ways--this leads to true intelligence.** There's nothing very technical in this book. It, too, is a society--of many small

---

[112] MT, 89 (Ch. 11). Ortega uses the Latin expression, *similia similibus* (similar things for similar things).

[113] MT, 89 (Ch. 11). Ortega's Egyptian ramp example is still part of current speculation. See Becky Little, "How Did Egyptians Build the Pyramids? Ancient Ramp Deepens Mystery," Nov. 12, 2018, https://www.history.com/news/ancient-egypt-pyramid-ramp-discovery .

[114] MT, 89 (Ch. 11).

[115] MT, 92 (Ch. 12).

[116] MT, 92-92 (Ch. 12).

[117] MT, 93 (Ch. 12).

ideas. Each by itself is only commonsense, yet when we join enough of them we can explain the strangest mysteries of mind.[118]

The method is clear: analytically break down the goal into its simplest component parts and then build up to the ultimate result.

Ortega sees in physics the exemplar of this method: "analysis and experimentation."[119] He ends his *Meditation on Technology* with an extended quotation of statistics illustrating the vast increase in productivity that technology has made possible. The quoted statistics concern the production of energy, the reduction of labor hours, and the output of physical products such as light bulbs and bricks.[120] Ortega would have been amazed but not surprised by Minsky's ambitious project for artificial intelligence. Ortega would not be surprised because of his intuition that technology is by nature unlimited.

---

[118] Marvin Minsky, *The Society of Mind* (New York: Simon & Schuster, 1985), p. 17 (Prologue; emphasis added).
[119] MT, 94 (Ch. 12).
[120] MT, 94-96 (Ch. 12).

Brief Conclusion

Ortega was a first-rate thinker and philosophical mind. That noteworthy ability is verified by the current relevance of his insights, although the insights date from 1933. Most importantly, Ortega's thoughts on technology encourage us to address the serious ethical and philosophical issues raised by artificial intelligence and by technology in general. The philosophical analysis of technology modelled by Ortega is a useful guide for those wrestling with these issues precisely because his philosophizing emphasizes the possibility of life projects that can maximize the value of technology for human well-being and happiness.

Author Oswald Sobrino is a doctoral student in Latin and Roman Studies at the University of Florida who is interested in philosophy and technology and is fluent in Spanish.

www.ingramcontent.com/pod-product-compliance
Lightning Source LLC
Chambersburg PA
CBHW060935050326
40689CB00013B/3100